THE
SAN FRANCISCO
EARTHQUAKE

Look for these and other exciting
World Disasters books:
Pompeii
The Black Death
The Titanic
The Dust Bowl
The Chicago Fire
The Armenian Earthquake
The Crash of '29

THE
SAN FRANCISCO
EARTHQUAKE

by James House and Bradley Steffens

Illustrations by Maurie Manning
and
Michael Spackman
Robert Caldwell
Randol Eagles

LUCENT
B·O·O·K·S

WORLD DISASTERS

Library of Congress Cataloging-in-Publication Data

House, James, 1940-, and Steffens, Bradley, 1955
    San Francisco earthquake/by James House and Bradley Steffens; illustrations by Maurie Manning.
      p. cm. — (World disasters)
    Bibliography: p.
    Includes index.
    Summary: An account of the earthquake of 1906 in San Francisco, during which fires began which raged unchecked over the city, virtually destroying it.
    ISBN 1-56006-003-4 : $12.95
    1. Earthquakes—California—San Francisco—History—20th century—Juvenile literature.   2. San Francisco (Calif.)—History—Juvenile literature.   [1. Earthquakes—California—San Francisco—History—20th century.   2. San Francisco (Calif.)—History.]
    I. Manning, Maurie, 1960-   ill.   II. Title.   III. Series.
F869.S357H68 1989   89-33558
979.4'61051-dc20   CIP
                                        AC

© Copyright 1989 Lucent Books, Inc.
Lucent Books, Inc., P.O. Box 289011, San Diego, California 92128-9011

Table of Contents

Preface

The World Disasters Series

World disasters have always aroused human curiosity. Whenever news of tragedy spreads, we want to learn more about it. We wonder how and why the disaster happened, how people reacted, and whether we might have acted differently. To be sure, disaster evokes a wide range of responses—fear, sorrow, despair, generosity, even hope. Yet from every great disaster, one remarkable truth always seems to emerge: in spite of death, pain, and destruction, the human spirit triumphs.

History is full of great disasters, which arise from a variety of causes. Earthquakes, floods, volcanic eruptions, and other natural events often produce widespread destruction. Just as often, however, people accidentally bring suffering and distress on themselves and other human beings. And many disasters have sinister causes, like human greed, envy, or prejudice.

The disasters included in this series have been chosen not only for their dramatic qualities, but also for their educational value. The reader will learn about the causes and effects of the greatest disasters in history. Technical concepts and interesting anecdotes are explained and illustrated in inset boxes.

But disasters should not be viewed in isolation. To enrich the reader's understanding, these books present historical information about the time period, and interesting facts about the culture in which each disaster occurred. Finally, they teach valuable lessons about human nature. More acts of bravery, cowardice, intelligence, and foolishness are compressed into the few days of a disaster than most people experience in a lifetime.

Dramatic illustrations and evocative narrative lure the reader to distant cities and times gone by. Readers witness the awesome power of an exploding volcano, the magnitude of a violent earthquake, and the hopelessness of passengers on a mighty ship passing to its watery grave. By reliving the events, the reader will see how disaster affects the lives of real people and will gain a deeper understanding of their sorrow, their pain, their courage, and their hope.

Introduction
"Almost" the Perfect City

San Francisco is one of the busiest seaports in the world, and it has often been called America's most beautiful city. Lying at the foot of the coastal mountains that overlook California's largest bay, this hilly city is rich with trees and has an abundance of flowers and greenery. The region enjoys a mild climate, ideal for the vineyards that cover the hills and valleys further inland. In many ways, this is an ideal location for a major city.

With its colorful history and architecture and its reputation for fine restaurants, nightclubs, and theaters, San Francisco is one of the most enjoyable cities in the country. Thousands of visitors come here every year, and most of the people who live here would not want to move anywhere else in the world.

However, there is one disturbing problem in this picturesque city with the "ideal" location. It is situated directly above the San Andreas Fault, a huge crack in the earth's surface formed by earthquakes, which regularly shake this region of California.

Most of the earthquakes are minor, and they cause little damage. But the people of San Francisco must live with the knowledge and constant fear that a major earthquake could strike at any time, like the quake that nearly destroyed the city in 1906.

In that year, on Wednesday, April 18, the largest earthquake in American history ripped through San Francisco. Streets buckled, and many buildings collapsed. But that was not the worst of it.

The earthquake caused gas pipes and oil barrels to break. It knocked down electric wires, and sparks from the broken wires started fires. Scattered fires quickly spread throughout the city and raged out of control for three days. By the time the fires were out, San Francisco had suffered the largest city fire in the history of the world.

Today whenever people in San Francisco speak of "the Quake," or "the Fire," they are referring to these events, which changed the face of their beautiful city forever. To know what the city was like then, we must go back in time to the days of San Francisco in 1906.

The San Francisco Earthquake's
Place in History

First American ship sails into San Francisco Bay—1799
Louisiana Purchase—1803
Major earthquake reported in San Francisco—1808

Mexico gains independence from Spain with California as part of the new republic—1821

Mexican War—1846-1848
Gold discovered at Sutter's Mill—1848
Volunteer fire department organized in San Francisco—1849
California becomes 31st state—1850
Disastrous fire in San Francisco causes $5 million in damage—1856
American Civil War—1861-1865
Official paid fire department formed in San Francisco—1866
Golden Spike completes transcontinental railroad—1869
Cable cars installed in San Francisco—1873

San Francisco lighted by electricity—1902
San Francisco Earthquake and Fire—1906

World War I—1914-1918

Golden Gate Bridge opens—1937
World War II—1939-1945

John F. Kennedy assassinated—1963

Neil Armstrong walks on the moon—1969

Ronald Reagan president of the U.S.—1981-1989

One
The City

With sails billowing and lines taut, the schooner *John A. Campbell* cut through the waves of the Pacific Ocean on Tuesday, April 17, 1906. It was headed for the calm waters of San Francisco Bay, which lay 150 miles (242 kilometers) to the east. After sailing through a narrow opening in the mountains, known as the Golden Gate, the ship would make its way to the docks of San Francisco, where it would take its place alongside dozens of other tall ships and steamers. There, dockworkers would unload the ship's cargo, moving it by hand, crane, and cart into one of the many huge brick warehouses in the city's waterfront district. Eventually, items from the *John A. Campbell* would be sold or traded, adding to San Francisco's wealth of commerce.

Trade from ships like the *John A. Campbell* had transformed San Francisco from a small village into the largest city in the western half of the United States. In just sixty years, the population had grown from a few hundred fur traders, soldiers, and mis-

sionaries to more than four hundred thousand sailors, dockworkers, factory workers, storekeepers, and professionals. Most had been drawn by the tremendous opportunities that had sprung up around the city's harbor, the busiest port on the West Coast.

Two factors had made San Francisco Bay the focal point for trade in California. The first factor was geography. The coast of California offers few protected harbors to ships bearing cargo from Europe and Asian countries like

the mining camps that lay within a hundred miles (160 kilometers) of San Francisco. With no railroad and few wagon train trails connecting California with the rest of the United States, the seas provided the fastest, most economical route to the gold rush.

Most of the people and supplies bound for California's gold fields passed through the Golden Gate and landed in San Francisco. Likewise, the gold found by the prospectors was sent to San Francisco to be kept safe in the city's banks or shipped to gold traders around the world.

Japan, China, and India. As Bartolomeo Ferrelo, the first European to explore the area, reported in 1543, the coast of California is lined with mountains "that rise to the sky, and against which the sea beats, and which appear as if they would fall on the ships."

Only three major inlets interrupt the coastline: Humboldt Bay, San Diego Bay, and San Francisco Bay. Of these, San Francisco Bay is by far the largest. Beyond the narrow opening known as the Golden Gate stretch 150 square miles (384 square kilometers) of placid waters. A peninsula closes off the bay from the south. On the eastern edge of the peninsula sandy flatlands gently rise from the water—an ideal place for docking. On this spot, traders had built San Francisco's waterfront.

The second factor that transformed San Francisco from a sleepy town into a bustling city was the discovery of gold at Sutter's Mill on the American River in 1848. When word of the discovery spread around the world, thousands of people decided to seek their fortunes in

WHERE IS SAN FRANCISCO?

San Francisco is one of the most important seaports on the West Coast of the United States. Located in northern California, it lies at the entrance to San Francisco Bay, the state's largest bay. Along with Oakland, Berkeley, Richmond, San Jose, and other cities, San Francisco is part of what is known as the Bay Area.

Of the more than one billion dollars worth of gold discovered in California before 1906, only a small fraction of it had been carried out of the state by the miners. Most of the gold had changed hands at least once in California, fueling a financial boom that dwarfed the actual take from the mines.

Owners of dry goods stores had profited first, selling picks, shovels, tents, food, and other necessities to miners. Some of these retailers had begun shipping goods inland to the miners and transporting gold out, becoming pioneers in the freight, mail, and banking businesses. The fortunes of several prominent San Francisco

THE GOLD RUSH

In January 1848, gold was discovered at Sutter's Mill on the American River near Sacramento, California. News of the discovery quickly spread across the country, and in 1849, thousands of people streamed into the rugged gold fields east of San Francisco. Mostly men, these prospectors became known as forty-niners because of the year in which most of them arrived.

The gold rush marked the real birth of San Francisco, a city whose population hadn't yet reached a thousand. The nearest seaport to the gold fields, it quickly grew into the business and transportation center of the gold rush. Most of the new residents lived in tents or hastily built shacks. General stores, land offices, and banks sprang up almost overnight. Millions of dollars worth of gold passed through San Francisco's banks, and by 1850, the city reached a population of twenty-five thousand.

families, including the Stanfords, Hopkinses, and Crockers, had begun in this fashion.

San Francisco's pioneer merchants and bankers also financed other growing industries, including lumber, ranching, railroads, and trade with the Orient. In 1868, the first transcontinental railroad was completed, linking San Francisco with the rest of the United States and bringing even more business to the city. Several eastern banks, including Adams and Company, opened branches in San

the financial district in what became known as Chinatown.

Only six blocks long and two blocks wide, Chinatown was the most densely populated section of the city. The Chinese population continued to grow while the boundaries of Chinatown remained the same. As a result, Chinese families crowded together, sometimes living twenty to thirty people to a room.

Italians, many of whom had been recruited by shipping companies, made up another prominent group of immigrants. The shipping companies often sent representatives to port cities in Italy to offer dockworkers free passage to America and guaranteed employment. In exchange, the workers promised to work for the company for several years.

Most of the Italian immigrants made their homes on Telegraph Hill, just north of the waterfront district. Italian clothing stores, hardware stores, and bakeries lined the streets. Grocers hung yards of spaghetti, macaroni, and sausages in their windows. One of the banks serving the Italian community was the new Bank of Italy, founded by A.P. Giannini. Eventually, it grew into the nation's largest bank, the Bank of America.

Once they had secured their fortunes, many wealthy Italians moved out of the Italian District, but many remained. The houses of the well-to-do, with their little gardens, looked like Mediterranean **villas**. Few Italian immigrants could afford to own their own homes, however. Most rented apartments in primitive wooden buildings, many of which were poorly ventilated and had no running water. Some families crowded into single rooms, without kitchen or bathroom facilities.

Francisco. By 1906, San Francisco was the financial capital of the West. Its financial district stretched for blocks along Montgomery Street, which was known as the Wall Street of the West.

As business boomed, thousands of workers flocked to the city seeking jobs. Among these were large groups of **immigrants** from China, Japan, Italy, and Russia. Each of these immigrant groups settled into separate neighborhoods in San Francisco.

Many of the Chinese and Japanese worked on the docks, in canneries, at cigar factories, and in shoe shops. Some Chinese fished for a living, and a few of the Japanese farmed. Chinese men were easy to spot on the street. They wore dark **tunics** and pants and had long braids that hung down their backs. Chinese children wore bright, shiny outfits and ornate hats. Nearly all of the Asians in San Francisco lived in a cluster of brick buildings to the west of

14

To the west of Telegraph Hill lies Russian Hill, named for the Russian immigrants that first settled there. By 1906, Russian Hill was also the home of many of the doctors, lawyers, teachers, and other professionals who had flocked to San Francisco to serve the growing population. Most of the homes were built of wood, in the decorative style popular during the **Victorian** era.

To the south of Russian Hill lies Nob Hill, the fashionable neighborhood of many of San Francisco's most prominent citizens. Many of the homes that dotted Nob Hill were built of brick, and even marble. Their stained-glass windows glittered in the sunlight, and their great **gables**, **turrets**, and spires stretched toward the sky.

The interiors of the Nob Hill homes were as elegant as any of their day. **Frescoes**, or paintings made on wet plaster, decorated the arched ceilings of the parlors and sitting rooms. In room after room, paintings by famous European artists hung on the walls,

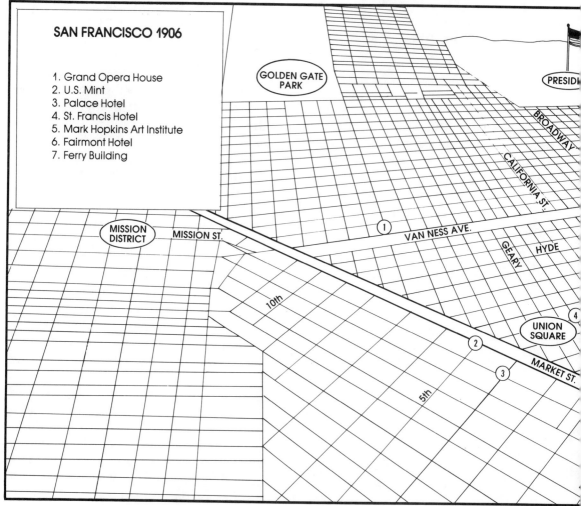

SAN FRANCISCO 1906

1. Grand Opera House
2. U.S. Mint
3. Palace Hotel
4. St. Francis Hotel
5. Mark Hopkins Art Institute
6. Fairmont Hotel
7. Ferry Building

marble sculptures rested on carved pedestals, and oriental carpets stretched across hardwood floors.

Crowning the hill was the Mark Hopkins mansion, built by the dry goods merchant who had helped form the Central Pacific Railroad. Although it had been the residence of the Hopkins family for many years, by 1906 the Hopkins Mansion had been given to the University of California at Berkeley. The University named the building the Mark Hopkins Art Institute and used

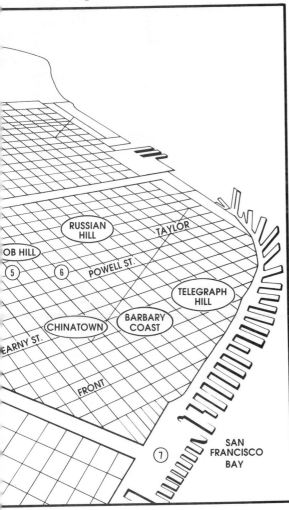

it to house a portion of the school's art collection.

Directly east of Nob Hill, at the foot of Telegraph Hill, was the most notorious section of the city, the Barbary Coast district. Named after the famous land of pirates, the Barbary Coast catered to the many sailors who put ashore in San Francisco. Centered on Pacific Street, the Barbary Coast consisted of block after block of saloons, dance halls, and **brothels**. All night, every night, the sound of orchestras, steam pianos, and gramophones blared out of windows and doors of its many night spots.

The Barbary Coast district, along with Chinatown, Telegraph Hill, Russian Hill, and Nob Hill, is located north of Market Street. This wide street runs east and west across the city, terminating at the Ferry Building on the eastern waterfront. In 1906, Market Street was a main thoroughfare for horse-drawn wagons, buggies, automobiles, and cable cars.

Many of San Francisco's most important buildings stood along Market Street, such as the Palace Hotel, where many important people, including Ulysses S. Grant, had stayed. The area south of Market Street was known simply as South of the Slot, referring to the metal slot in the street that housed the cable for the cable car system. South of the Slot was a working-class neighborhood. The modest houses and apartment buildings that lined its streets were framed with wood and covered with **clapboard** siding. Wooden homes also filled the adjacent neighborhood, called the Mission District. At the center of this district was the old Spanish mission of St. Francis, the saint for whom San Francisco was named.

Despite their **ethnic** and economic diversity, most San Franciscans shared a great civic pride. The citizens had created the most refined city west of the Mississippi. Like the large cities in the East, San Francisco boasted paved streets, gas street lights, large water and sewer systems, extensive electric and telephone services, and an excellent fire department. Its schools and libraries were considered the finest in California. The city had five newspapers and two literary journals.

On the western edge of the city lay a great public park known as Golden Gate Park. In the 1890s, more than 1,016 acres of sand dunes had been transformed into a lush retreat. Visitors to the park found wide lawns, well-tended flower gardens, and small forests of eucalyptus, Monterey pine, and cypress trees. Men dressed in knickers and high-necked sweaters and women wearing divided skirts, leggings, and **tams** rode bicycles through the park. Families picnicked on the lawns, listened to outdoor orchestras, and, occasionally, watched balloonists soar into the air and then parachute to the ground.

The park did not offer the only entertainment in town, however. Three amusement parks, all named The Chutes, offered San Franciscans water-slide rides, theatrical shows, and arcade

amusements. Downtown, the Orpheum Theatre presented vaudeville shows at a price of ten cents per evening. The city also offered a wealth of serious theater and opera. On Tuesday, April 17, 1906, the Columbia Theatre was presenting Victor Herbert's *Babes In Toyland*, the Tivoli was staging *Miss Timidity*, and the Majestic offered *Who Goes There?*

The event of the evening, however, was being held at the Grand Opera House. There, three thousand of San Francisco's elite paid up to ten dollars per seat to hear Enrico Caruso sing the part of Don Jose in Bizet's opera, *Carmen*.

Caruso had been in the news a great deal that week. It was the great Italian opera star's first visit to San Francisco, and the city's newspaper reporters were eager to record his reactions to their city. In addition, Caruso's hometown, Naples, Italy, had been struck by an eruption of the great volcano, Mt. Vesuvius. Two thousand people had already died, and thousands more were homeless. Reporters pressed Caruso for some insight into the disaster.

"I cannot tell you what Vesuvius is really like," said Caruso. "No man can. It is the most frightening experience of all."

Caruso had been reluctant to join New York's Metropolitan Opera Company on its trip to San Francisco. He feared the "wild West," and had asked the company's management to allow him to return home to Naples for the summer. When management refused, Caruso purchased a gun and fifty rounds of ammunition to protect himself.

After hearing the news that the eruption of Mt. Vesuvius threatened Naples, Caruso viewed his tour differently. Gazing out the window of his opulent suite in the Palace Hotel on the evening of April 17, 1906, the tenor felt relieved to be in San Francisco. He told his conductor, Alfred Hertz, "Perhaps it was God's will after all that I should come this far."

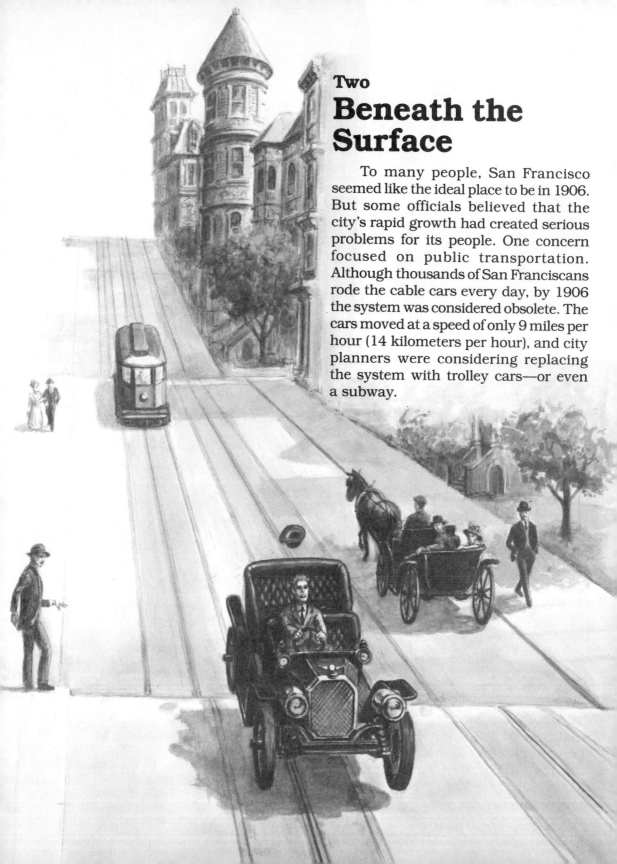

Two
Beneath the Surface

To many people, San Francisco seemed like the ideal place to be in 1906. But some officials believed that the city's rapid growth had created serious problems for its people. One concern focused on public transportation. Although thousands of San Franciscans rode the cable cars every day, by 1906 the system was considered obsolete. The cars moved at a speed of only 9 miles per hour (14 kilometers per hour), and city planners were considering replacing the system with trolley cars—or even a subway.

Another problem was the layout of the city itself. The streets spread out in orderly grids, but this organization did not suit the hilly terrain of San Francisco. Instead of gradually winding up the sides of hills, San Francisco's streets attacked the hills directly. These straight, steep streets were difficult to climb by foot, in wagons, and even in automobiles. For drivers, descending the steep roads was extremely dangerous. Runaway wagons and automobiles were a common sight. The steep hills also created pumping problems for the city's water lines and drainage problems for its sewer lines.

This was not only an inconvenience for citizens, but also a cause for growing concern. In many parts of the city, water pressure was inadequate for fighting fires. With all the wooden buildings in the city, fire was a constant threat. Indeed, six times in its history, fire had destroyed all or most of the city.

In the fifty years prior to 1906, San Francisco's excellent fire department had prevented a major fire, but each year more people had crowded into the city. As houses and other buildings were hastily built to accommodate the growing population, the danger of a major fire increased. Overcrowding also meant that more lives than ever would be endangered by a fast-spreading fire.

After having burned to the ground several times, much of San Francisco's downtown section had been rebuilt with brick and stone to resist fire. A few buildings, like the Palace Hotel, had been designed to be fireproof. Each of the hotel's eight hundred rooms contained modern fire detectors. In addition, a team of hotel watchmen checked each floor every thirty-four minutes. In the hotel's basement stood a huge water tank, equipped with three high-pressure pumps. Another seven water tanks were located on the roof. These tanks were connected to 5 miles (8 kilometers) of piping with 350 hoses for fighting fires. Even if the city's water supply were shut down, crews at the Palace Hotel had plenty of water to fight a fire.

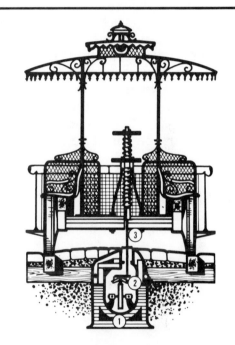

THE CABLE CARS

Cable cars were first used in the mining industry to haul ore out of deep mine shafts. Andrew Hollidie was the first to use this technology for city transportation, opening the city's first cable car company in 1873. Workers dug slots (1) in the streets and lay thick steel cables (2) in these slots. Cars were attached (3) to the cables, which were pulled by huge, steam-powered pulleys.

Cable cars were a practical solution to the problem of transportation over the city's many hills which were too steep for horse-drawn trolleys. Today, cable cars still provide transportation in San Francisco, and have long been one of the city's most popular tourist attractions.

The danger of fire was much greater outside the downtown area. To get as much as they could out of the land they owned, developers had crammed each square block with shops, houses, and apartments. South of the Slot, they had even filled in Willow and Mission Creeks with garbage and loose fill dirt to create extra lots on which to build. On the east side of town, developers had extended the city six full blocks by filling the bay with loose dirt at the city's edge.

Almost all the buildings located outside the downtown area had been framed with wood and covered with clapboard. Most had wooden shingles on their roofs. The danger from fire was obvious. In an article entitled "Eastern Impressions of San Francisco" that appeared in May, 1872, a reporter for an eastern newspaper made a grim prediction:

> With the fearful destruction recently wreaked in Chicago by the dread demon fire vivid in my mind, it is impossible to walk through the streets of San Francisco without feeling a presentiment of an even more terrible fate in store for this great metropolis. One is forced...to look upon it as a doomed city, and the mind cannot help but paint itself a horrible picture of the lapping flames leaping from one frail tinder-box to another, until [the whole] prosperous city is swept from existence.... It needs no gift of prophecy to predict the future, for it is inevitable.

THE FIRE FIGHTERS OF SAN FRANCISCO

Since its earliest days, San Francisco has been subject to fires. Perhaps that is why San Franciscans have always shown a strong interest in their fire department. Until 1866, all the fire stations in the city were manned by volunteer fire fighters. Many statues and monuments, including Coit Tower, one of the city's most famous landmarks, were built in memory of these volunteers.

Formed in 1866, the official, "paid" San Francisco Fire Department became the pride of the city. With their brass steamers polished until they glistened, and their beautiful thoroughbred horses groomed to perfection, members of the fire department appeared regularly at the city's many parades and other civic events. The people of the city recognized that for the forty years before the quake, the fire fighters defied all odds and kept the city from suffering a major fire.

Not only did the crowded neighborhoods of San Francisco provide miles of fuel for fire, but also the city's water supply was poorly equipped to handle a major fire. In a report published in October of 1905, the National Board of Fire Underwriters stated that San Francisco's water system was "inadequate to meet the demands for water flow necessary to fight a *conflagration*." The report declared:

> *San Francisco has violated all underwriting traditions and precedents by not burning up. That it has not done so is largely due to the vigilance of the Fire Department, which cannot be relied upon indefinitely to stave off the inevitable.*

The board's report shocked many city officials, but not Dennis Sullivan, chief of the San Francisco Fire Department. He was proud of his department, but he knew that the valiant efforts of his men would not be enough to save the city forever. Long before the board had made its report public, Sullivan had asked leaders at city hall for money to improve the department's fire-fighting capabilities.

Sullivan wanted money to rebuild and enlarge the city's *cisterns*, or basins that catch and hold rainwater. While dozens of cisterns had been built early in the city's history, they had been neglected and allowed to dry up. Sullivan also proposed linking the city's hydrant system to the bay to use this unlimited supply of seawater to fight fires.

For months, city officials had ignored Sullivan's pleas. But after the release of the Board of Underwriter's report, Mayor Eugene Schmitz called a meeting of concerned citizens to discuss what could be done to prepare for future emergencies. The meeting was held on April 17, 1906, at the Hall of Justice. Chief Sullivan was scheduled to present his proposals the next day.

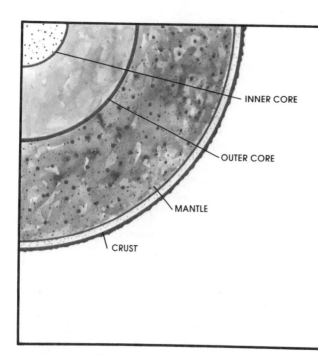

INNER CORE

OUTER CORE

MANTLE

CRUST

WHAT CAUSES EARTHQUAKES?

The interior of the earth has three distinct layers: the *inner core, outer core,* and *mantle.* The inner core is a mass of solid iron. This is surrounded by the outer core, a liquid layer of extremely hot, molten iron. Around the outer core is the mantle, a 1,500-mile-deep (2,415-kilometer) layer of molten rock which can be quite fluid.

The mantle is surrounded by the earth's *crust,* a hardened layer of rock that is only about 20 miles thick (32 kilometers). It is the movement of the solid crust on the liquid mantle that causes earthquakes.

The crust is broken into seven large *tectonic plates* and several smaller ones. Molten rock rising up from the mantle forces these plates to move. As they move, the plates sometimes grind slowly past one another. At other times, two plates collide, or the edge of one may slip over the other. The contact between plates unleashes strong vibrations, or earthquakes, that crack and deform the earth's surface.

Police Officer Leonard Ingham was also deeply concerned about the city's fire danger. Ingham did not take a public stand on the fire prevention issue, but he was obsessed by a private fear. Over and over in the spring of 1906, Patrolman Ingham had been awakened by the same nightmare. He dreamed that a fire started in the Mission District and swept up Market Street, burning the Palace Hotel and many other important buildings. On the night of April 16, the dream had been so vivid that Officer Ingham decided to tell the chief of police about it. Ingham had been given an appointment to speak with the chief at 9:00 A.M., April 18.

In the meantime, he decided to take action to protect his own family against the fire he believed was coming. Less than twenty-four hours before his appointment with the chief, Ingham walked into the office of the Hartford Fire Insurance Company and asked to buy an insurance policy for his home. The company's agent, Adam Gilliland, gladly obliged. He drew up a two-thousand-dollar policy to cover Ingham's home against loss by fire.

As Gilliland worked on the policy, Officer Ingham told the insurance agent about his dream. Gilliland was fascinated. After Ingham left his office, Gilliland dropped his normal duties and began to do some research. After several hours, he discovered something that seemed to make Ingham's nightmare more believable.

Gilliland found that in 1895 the distinguished *geologist* Andrew Lawson had discovered a huge *fault,* or break in the earth's *crust,* that ran directly beneath the city of San Francisco. Lawson claimed that movement along this fault had caused earthquakes in the past, and it would probably do so again. A serious earthquake, Gilliland knew, could break gas pipes and cause the kind of fire that Officer Ingham had dreamed about.

Indeed, San Francisco had been rocked by earthquakes throughout its history. In 1865, a strong earthquake had damaged city hall and had broken street posts, water lines, and gas pipes along Market Street. Three years later, a much bigger quake had ripped through the city. Entire buildings had fallen in dusty heaps. Chimneys had crashed through the ceilings of several homes. *Facades* had torn loose from some buildings and crashed to the streets below.

Two more strong quakes shook the city in 1892 and 1898. Smaller quakes rattled windows and jiggled dishes almost every year. But most San Franciscans preferred an occasional buckling of the ground to the blizzards, hurricanes, and tornadoes that regularly killed hundreds of people in the East and Midwest. In 1906, however, few San Franciscans had lived in the city long enough to remember the last great quake in 1868. None could anticipate the fury about to be released far beneath the earth's surface.

LIVING NEAR THE EDGE

Most earthquakes occur along the edges between two tectonic plates. One of these edges lies directly beneath the state of California. The contact between the two plates wrenches, twists, and snaps the ground above them, causing the ground to shift and crack. The places where these shifts and breaks in the ground occur are called *faults*. Discovered by Andrew Lawson in 1895, the largest fault in California is the San Andreas Fault, which has been traced over 720 miles (1150 kilometers) and extends another 300 miles (480 kilometers) or more into the Pacific Ocean.

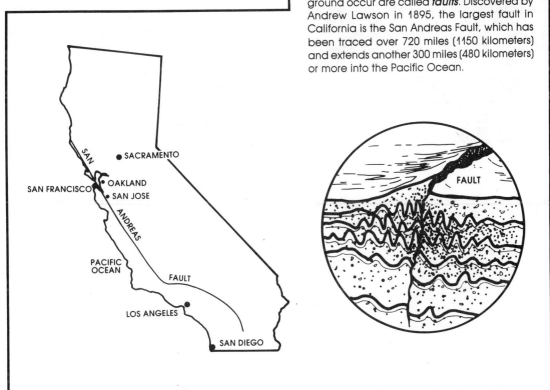

rest of the cast. At about 1:00 A.M. on Wednesday, April 18, Caruso told Antonio Scotti that he wanted "to hunt some spaghetti and fun," and the two headed for Zinkand's Restaurant.

Outside, the weather was calm, but the night was not entirely peaceful. Dogs howled. Here and there, cabbies fought to control their skittish horses, which stamped their hoofs on the cobblestones and reared up for no apparent reason.

At 2:00 A.M., James Hopper, a reporter for the *Call*, one of San Francisco's daily newspapers, had just completed his account of Caruso's performance and was walking down Post Street toward his room at the Neptune Hotel. As he passed a livery stable, he was startled by the "sudden, shrill cry" of a horse. Later, he recalled:

> *I asked a stableman lolling in the darkened doorway what was the matter. 'Restless tonight! Don't know why!' he answered. And then, with my head poked in, I heard the thunder of a score of hoofs crashing...against the walls.*

Shortly before 5:00 A.M., Patrolman Ingham suddenly awoke. This time, it was not his nightmare that had awakened him, but a commotion outside. A milk cart clattered in the darkness as the driver tried to calm his excited horse.

A few blocks away, another policeman, Sergeant Jesse Cook, stopped to chat with a produce merchant at the corner of Washington and Davis. It was 5:12 A.M.. The sun had begun to lighten the eastern sky, and it looked like another beautiful day in one of the world's most beautiful cities.

Three
Shock

Caruso's appearance at the Grand Opera House on Tuesday, April 17, 1906, was a triumph. When the performance ended, the audience clapped and cheered for several minutes. Nine times the fiery tenor returned to the stage to acknowledge the applause.

At about midnight, Caruso returned to the Palace Hotel to celebrate with the

A hundred and fifty miles (242 kilometers) out to sea, the crew that was on duty on the *John A. Campbell* were going about their morning duties. The lookout scanned the water ahead for signs of trouble. On the bridge, Captain Svenson reviewed his ship's position. Suddenly, the bow of the *John A. Campbell* shot out of the water. The entire three-thousand-ton ship rose into midair, then fell back into the water with a crash.

The disturbance awakened the crew members who had been sleeping. The startled sailors rushed on deck to see what the ship had struck. Clinging to the ship's rails, the crew searched the water for a reef, a whale, anything.

They saw nothing.

They looked to their captain for an explanation. Captain Svenson just shrugged. He pulled out his log book and wrote:

Sudden motion, unexplained. The shock felt as if the vessel struck...and then appeared to drag over soft ground.

Although Captain Svenson did not realize it at the time, he and his crew had passed over the **focus** of the largest earthquake to rock California in recorded history. Far beneath the ocean's floor, the San Andreas Fault had slipped, sending out shock waves in all directions. One of the waves had slammed into the bottom of the *John A. Campbell* and pushed the ship right out of the water. Other shock waves were headed toward shore, buckling the earth as they moved toward San Francisco.

On Washington Street, Sergeant Cook actually saw the earth's crust ripple as the shock waves ripped through the city:

> *The whole street was **undulating**. It was as if the waves of the ocean were coming towards me, billowing as they came.*

A few blocks away, John Barrett, the city desk news editor for another San Francisco daily newspaper, the *Examiner*, stood on the sidewalk with his colleagues. As the earthquake hit, Barrett felt the sidewalk pitch and roll, like the deck of a ship:

> *It was as though the earth was slipping away under our feet. There was a sickening sway, and we were all flat on our faces.*

SEISMIC WAVES

Once jerked out of shape by an earthquake, rocks lurch back toward their original position. This causes ***seismic waves*** of energy to go out in every direction. These waves of energy shake the ground many miles away from the earthquake's origin.

As they travel through the ground, two different kinds of seismic waves can be distinguished. *Primary waves* travel the fastest, and move in a straight line from the origin of the earthquake, alternately pushing and pulling the ground like an accordion. *Secondary waves* move in an "s" pattern. They travel slightly slower than primary waves and cause the ground to ripple both up and down and from side to side.

Once these waves reach the surface, they slow down and change their patterns of movement. Some whip the ground back and forth horizontally. Others churn the rock and soil in their path.

PRIMARY WAVES

SECONDARY WAVES

In his room at the Neptune Hotel, James Hopper was jarred awake like thousands of other terrified San Franciscans. He wrote:

> *I awoke to the city's destruction. Right away it was incredible, the violence of the 'quake....It pounced upon the earth like a bulldog.*

Hopper rushed to his window, shouting, "It's incredible, incredible." Below, the hotel's fire escape tore loose from the wall and crashed to the shaking earth. Hopper looked out over the city, and he never forgot what he saw:

> *I heard the roar of bricks coming down, and twisted girders, and at the same time saw a pale crescent moon in the green sky. The St. Francis Hotel was waving to and fro with a swing as violent and exaggerated as a tree in a tempest. Then the rear of my building, for three stories upward, fell. The mass struck a series of little wooden houses in the alley below. I saw them crash in like emptied eggs, the bricks passing through the roofs as though through tissue paper.*

A mining engineer, John B. Farish, described what it was like to be inside the St. Francis Hotel:

> *I was awakened by a loud rumbling noise which might be compared to the mixed sounds of a strong wind rushing through a forest and breaking of waves against a cliff. In less time than it takes to tell, a **concussion**...shook the building to its foundations and then began a series of the liveliest motions imaginable, accompanied by a creaking, grinding, rasping sound, followed by tremendous crashes as the cornices of adjoining buildings and chimneys tottered to the ground.*

Downtown, the brick and plaster exterior of city hall peeled away from the building's metal frame and crashed into the street. Throughout the city, church bells clanged uncontrollably.

Still lying on the moving ground, John Barrett watched nearby buildings "dancing" on their foundations. He recalled that the streets were a shambles:

> *Trolley tracks were twisted, their wires down, wriggling like serpents, flashing blue sparks all the time. From some of the holes water was spurting; from others, gas.*

Across the city, the shoddy workmanship of years before wreaked unexpected havoc. Unbraced brick walls crumbled. Houses built on loose fill dirt above Mission and Willow Creeks whipped back and forth, then twisted off their foundations or simply collapsed. As hastily built wooden structures writhed above the rolling ground, the nails that held them together wrenched free, squealing loudly. One San Franciscan compared the noise to "thousands of violins, all at discord."

On Bush Street, smokestacks broke loose from the roof of the California Hotel and smashed through the roof of the fire station next door. At that very moment, Fire Chief Dennis Sullivan, who lived in the station house, was rushing toward the door of his wife's bedroom. The falling bricks punched a hole in the floor ahead of him. The chief and his wife plunged three stories to the ground. Mrs. Sullivan was not hurt, but her husband was. The man who had spent his career

preparing for just such a disaster lay unconscious on a pile of debris, unable to help anyone.

The shaking lasted for forty seconds, then stopped. Silence filled the streets. Everyone waited, wondering if the earthquake was over.

After a pause of ten seconds, the earth shuddered again.

In the Mission District, the wooden-framed Valencia Hotel collapsed, crushing dozens of occupants. Water from a broken water main began to seep through the debris, drowning many who had survived the fall. Several other hotels South of the Slot, including the Brunswick, Denver, and Cosmopolitan, were knocked flat.

Downtown, well-built structures, like the Ferry Building and the U.S. Mint, withstood the shaking fairly well. The Palace Hotel, with its 12-foot (4-meter) pillar foundations and reinforced brick walls, suffered little structural damage, but inside the hotel, the scene was chaotic. Plaster and chandeliers fell from ceilings. Bureaus skittered across hardwood floors as if on ice.

After fifteen seconds, the second

The effects of the earthquake on a San Francisco neighborhood.

tremor stopped. Once more, a hush fell over the city. Again people waited, but this time nothing happened. To James Hopper, the calm was as frightening as the chaos:

> *Throughout the long quaking, I had not heard a cry, not a sound, not a sob, not a whisper. And now, when the roar of crumbling buildings was over, and only a brick fell here and there, this silence continued, and it was an awful thing.*

Brigadier General Frederick Funston, commander of the U.S. Army forces stationed at the *presidio* in San Francisco, also was struck by the quiet that gripped the city. As he looked out over the city from his home on Nob Hill, Funston noticed that "there came not a single sound, no shrieking of whistles, no clanging of bells."

The absence of ringing bells disturbed those who were familiar with the city's emergency systems. Officials guessed that the first instinct for many survivors would be to summon help by pulling fire alarms, but no such bells sounded. Fire fighters at the central alarm station in Chinatown soon discovered the awful truth. The tremors had broken 556 of the 600 wet-cell batteries that powered the city's central fire alarm system. Communication between San Francisco's citizens and its fire department had been wiped out.

In the streets, men, women, and children stood gaping at the destruction around them. Some men wore full beards of shaving lather on their faces. Children clutched their favorite stuffed animals or blankets. Most people were dressed in nightshirts, or less. Gradually, people began to notice each other, and a few exchanged embarrassed smiles.

Here and there, the cries of those trapped in wreckage rose through the dusty air. Those who could move hurried to help those who could not. Many were momentarily stopped by jammed doors. The quake had knocked house after house out of alignment, and door frames had closed onto the doors like vises.

James Hopper dressed quickly and

hurried toward his office at the *Call*, taking notes as he went:

> The streets were full of people, half-clad, dishevelled, but silent, absolutely silent, as if suddenly they had become speechless idiots. I went down Post Street towards the center of town, and in the morning's garish light I saw many men and women with gray faces. No one spoke. All of them had a singular hurt expression—not one of physical pain, but rather one of injured sensibilities, as if some trusted friend had suddenly wronged them, or as if someone had been rude to them.

At the Palace Hotel, the conductor of the Metropolitan Opera, Alfred Hertz, rushed to the room of Enrico Caruso. He found the great tenor sitting upright in bed, weeping hysterically. Caruso feared that the shock of the earthquake had ruined his voice. Hertz opened a window and coaxed Caruso over to it. Tapping on the sill as if it were a conductor's podium, Hertz commanded the opera star to sing. The sound of the tenor's rich voice cascaded to the street below, mingling with the cries of the injured. Ironically, one of those who heard the opera star, Horatio Hovey, interpreted the brief concert as Caruso's "best and bravest" performance, "an attempt on the singer's part to show the world that at least he had not been scared."

Caruso's was not the only odd behavior witnessed in San Francisco that morning. A man in Union Square Park was seen trying to read the inscription on a monument through eyeglasses, the lenses of which had been knocked out by the earthquake. Immediately after the quake, an undertaker was seen carefully polishing the handles of a coffin as chaos swirled around him.

This statue fell from the second-story ledge of a Stanford University building.

As James Hopper made his way downtown, he dashed inside a building to help a man he saw stranded on the third floor. Hopper scrambled up the stairs "over piles of plaster and laths," but when he reached the third floor, he saw something that made him forget about the man:

I came to a piece of room in which I found a bed covered with debris. A slim white hand and wrist reached out of the debris, like an appeal. I threw off the stuff, and found a woman underneath, still alive, a little, slender thing, whom I had no trouble carrying down to the sidewalk, where someone put her in an express wagon. I went back with another man and we found a second woman, whom we took down on a door. There was another woman in another corner, covered by a pile of bricks. She was dead.

By this time, so many curious onlookers had arrived on the scene that a policeman had to disperse the crowd. Yet Hopper remained in the building, puzzled by a sound he could not explain:

I could hear a mysterious wailing somewhere in the back. Finally, I located it on the second floor. A strip of the hallway still remained along the right wall. I followed it till I came to a place where the whole hall was intact, and there, on a platform amid the ruins, a woman with long dishevelled hair was pacing to and fro, repeating in a long, drawn-out wail, over and over again, 'Oh, my husband is dead, and a young man is dead, and a woman is dead; oh, my husband is dead and a young man is dead and a woman is dead.'

'Where is your husband?' we roared in her ear, for she seemed unable to hear us. She pointed toward the back. We went toward the back and came to an abrupt end of the hall.

Hopper and the other men found a bed completely buried in bricks. They began clearing the rubble away as fast as they could:

> *Above us the walls of the homicidal building towered. After a while, a fireman joined us. He seemed stupefied, and like us began to pick up bricks one by one. Finally another fireman came and called him. 'Come on, Bill,' he said. 'There's fires.'*
>
> *They went off, and then, after we had worked a time longer, a red-headed youth who was digging with us said, 'What's de use of digging out those that's dead?'*
>
> *His remark struck us as being so profoundly true that without another word, we all quit.*

Standing outside his home on Dolores Street, Leonard Ingham noticed tongues of flame rising from the rubble. He told his wife to pack a few things, then take a ferry out of the city. In the gathering light of day, Patrolman Ingham saw his nightmare coming true.

San Francisco residents view fires north of Market Street.

Four
Inferno

Immediately after the earthquake, sparks rained from broken power lines across San Francisco. Gas pipes, buried in mountains of debris, leaked fuel. Splintered wood from collapsed buildings lay like kindling for block after block. It was a deadly combination. Within minutes of the earthquake, fifty fires had broken out across the city.

Most of these fires were quickly stamped out, smothered with blankets, or beaten down with shovels. Horse-drawn fire engines raced toward the larger fires. But over and over, the same scene was repeated. One fire fighter would thread a hose onto a hydrant. Another would crank open the valve. The men holding the hose would brace themselves, but nothing would happen. Instead of spewing a great stream of water, the hose would spit out a muddy trickle, then stop. The firemen would rush to another hydrant, but the result would be the same. They soon realized that the city's water mains were broken.

At 7:00 A.M., the acting fire chief, John Dougherty, told Mayor Schmitz the bad news. The hydrants were useless. The fire fighters had begun pumping water from the sewer lines and the twenty-three cisterns that still held water, but it would not be enough to stop the flames.

The fires Dougherty and Schmitz knew about were burning north of Market Street and moving southward. The fire chief and the mayor quickly agreed on a plan. The fire department would attempt to save the major buildings that lined Market Street, and they would use the street as a *firebreak*. Because the street was wide and was lined with brick and stone buildings that would resist the flames, Dougherty believed the fires could be kept from spreading past Market Street. Fire fighters from many different engine houses began to connect their hoses together. They built hoses long enough to pump seawater from the bay to dampen the buildings that lined the great boulevard.

What Schmitz and Dougherty did not realize was that several fires were already burning South of the Slot. The plan for saving Market Street was doomed. By 9:00 A.M., one landmark building after another exploded into flame. The Grand Opera House, where Caruso had performed the night before, was destroyed. The Call Building, where James Hopper had typed out his review of Caruso's performance, soon followed.

Shortly after 9:00 A.M., the city received another blow. Another fire started just north of Market Street, but far west of the downtown fires. This fire became known as the "Ham-and-Eggs" fire because it was believed to have been started by an unknown woman who had started cooking breakfast for her family at a stove that fed into a broken chimney. This fire quickly spread east, toward the downtown fires. Later, the flames turned south, jumping Market Street and joining up with the wall of flame that was moving up from South of the Slot.

On Market Street, crowds gathered to watch the fire fighters try to save the tall buildings that lined the boulevard. Each time, the same thing would happen. First, sparks would land on the roof. Then the fire would burn through the roof to the topmost story. The fire fighters would enter the building and run their hoses up the stairs to try to stop the blaze. The heat from the fire would cause the air inside to expand until it blew out the windows, sending a shower of glass to the streets below. The draft of fresh air would feed the flames, and fire fighters would be forced to retreat. Then the whole process would begin all over again.

Many people thought the outcome might be different at the Palace Hotel, with its great reserves of water and advanced fire-fighting equipment. For six hours, fire fighters dampened the roof and held off the flames. For many who watched, the American flag that waved atop the Palace became a symbol of the city's undying spirit. Several times, sparks from nearby buildings ignited the flag, but each time the banner refused to burn. Late in the afternoon, the tanks

within the Palace ran dry. Fire fighters reluctantly abandoned the building, then paused to watch as the Palace, too, began to burn.

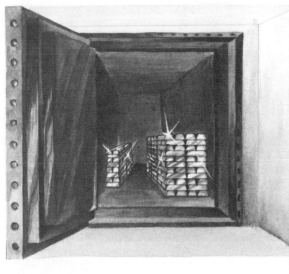

"SAVE THE MINT!"

In 1906, the United States Mint in San Francisco was one of only five locations in the country where coins and currency were made. Both the equipment for making money and the money stored in vaults in the building were quite valuable, and heavily guarded. To further protect this important operation, the building that housed the Mint was solid brick and designed to resist theft and fire.

In spite of the design, on Wednesday, April 18, the Mint caught fire. At the time, about $100 million was stored in its vaults. Fortunately, there were tanks of water stored in the basement for fire safety. For seven hours, fire fighters and soldiers from the sixth infantry fought to save the building. Fortunately, the fire fighters were able to pump enough water by hand to extinguish the fire and to wet down the roof and walls to prevent it from catching fire again. Many of the buildings around it burned to the ground, but the United States Mint and its millions were saved.

EARTHQUAKES AND FIRES

Some materials have a low *ignition point*, and require relatively little heat to catch fire. Other materials require more heat, and don't ignite as easily. Wood, coal, and oil all have low ignition points. This makes them good fuels.

When buildings collapse in an earthquake, many of these materials are exposed. Wooden walls and beams splinter and fall into piles along with furniture, bedding, clothing, and other flammable materials. Pipes, barrels, and storage tanks full of gas, oil, and other fuels often break and spring leaks. All these fuels are easily ignited by sparks from broken power lines and gas-lamps, and can cause fires throughout the area damaged by an earthquake.

Once fires are started they can be difficult to put out. Alarm systems may be out of order. Fire stations may be damaged, and streets leading to the fires are often blocked by debris.

As fire raged through the city, Mayor Schmitz issued a proclamation intended to prevent **looting** and crime. It gave police the authority to "shoot to kill" anyone caught looting. Knowing that even a few dozen drunken citizens could add to the chaos, Schmitz instructed Jeremiah Dinan, San Francisco's chief of police, to close every establishment that sold liquor. He also believed that the general disorder would be an invitation for some people to loot abandoned businesses. Intending to restore order in the city, he sent the following telegram to the Mare Island Naval Station:

EARTHQUAKE. TOWN ON FIRE.
SEND MARINES AND TUGS.

As it turned out, Schmitz's telegram was not needed. Brigadier General Funston had already ordered his troops stationed at the presidio to report to the chief of police at the Hall of Justice on Portsmouth Square.

Neither General Funston nor Mayor Schmitz actually had the authority to order troops into the city, but when Police Chief Dinan led the first troops through the streets of San Francisco, most citizens welcomed them. Standing guard with bayonets fixed to the ends of their rifles, the soldiers gave a sense of order to a city that was growing more chaotic by the minute. Businesspeople were able to leave their buildings without fear that looters might steal their merchandise. Firemen were able to concentrate on fighting fires instead of controlling crowds. Many citizens simply took comfort from knowing that someone appeared to be in charge of the situation.

PROCLAMATION
BY THE MAYOR

The Federal Troops, the members of the Regular Police Force and all Special Police Officers have been authorized by me to KILL any and all persons found engaged in Looting or in the Commission of Any Other Crime.

I have directed all the Gas and Electric Lighting Co.'s not to turn on Gas or Electricity until I order them to do so. You may therefore expect the city to remain in darkness for an indefinite time.

I request all citizens to remain at home from darkness until daylight every night until order is restored.

I WARN all Citizens of the danger of fire from Damaged or Destroyed Chimneys, Broken or Leaking Gas Pipes or Fixtures, or any like cause.

E. E. SCHMITZ, Mayor

Dated, April 18, 1906

Proclamation issued April 18, 1906

By Wednesday night, the day's many fires had joined into two giant fronts. One fire was sweeping north and west from downtown, toward Nob Hill. The other fire, south of Market, was burning straight west, toward the Mission District.

Without water, all the firemen could do was use dynamite to destroy buildings in the fire's path, hoping to create a break that the flames could not cross. Unfortunately, the fire department had no experience with dynamite, and the results were disastrous. The explosions hurled burning cinders in every direction, igniting other buildings that had not been threatened by fire.

One place the fire fighters tried to create a firebreak was on Kearny Street, at the edge of Chinatown. There, a dynamite explosion sent flaming bedding hurtling through the air toward the roof of a brick building across the street. The roof caught fire, and Chinatown

FIGHTING FIRES WITH NO WATER

In San Francisco, the broken water mains were a serious problem. The only alternative to putting the fires out was to create *firebreaks*, or areas in the path of a fire where all flammable material has been removed. Without fuel to burn, the fire dies out.

Unfortunately, most of the firebreaks created by fire fighters in San Francisco were unsuccessful because the fires were big enough to jump right over them. Also, firefighters using dynamite to destroy buildings and create the firebreaks had little experience with explosives. Often they accidentally started new fires that spread out of control.

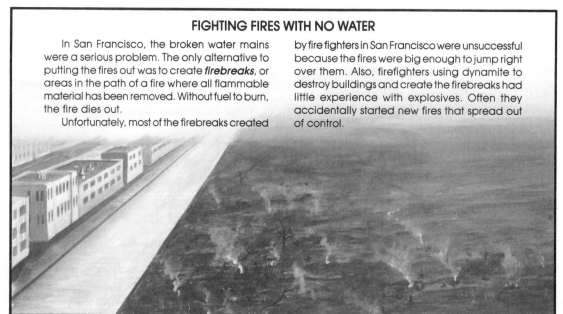

began to burn. By the next morning, the entire neighborhood was gone.

By the end of the day, more than one hundred thousand people were homeless. Many, including Enrico Caruso, hurried toward Golden Gate Park. Some pulled steamer trunks that had roller skates nailed to their bottoms. Others pushed baby buggies filled with household articles. A few men carried bureaus and other furniture on their backs. Others pushed upright pianos down the city streets.

As night fell, the flames lit the sky above San Francisco. People in towns 50 miles (80 kilometers) away said the fire gave off enough light to "read a newspaper at midnight."

As the fire ate its way through the city's great storehouse of materials, it changed color with the different materials it consumed. Henry Lafler, a writer for *McClure's Magazine*, reported:

All colors and shades were there. Here, for a moment, showed a pale, clear yellow, then again a fiery red. There were perfect blues, there was violet, green, and rose yellow. Then would come dark, sinister, demoniac hues, hateful as hell.

Fire fighters had hoped to hold the northern front of the fire at Powell Street before it consumed the Fairmont Hotel and the fine mansions of Nob Hill. Union Square, an open park one square block in size, offered a natural firebreak, and the firemen were able to coax water from an old cistern nearby. For two hours, fire fighters were able to hold the line there. Then, at 3:00 A.M., a few sparks flew over the street and settled on the wooden spire of an old church. The building exploded into flames, and many of the city's finest homes and historic buildings were doomed.

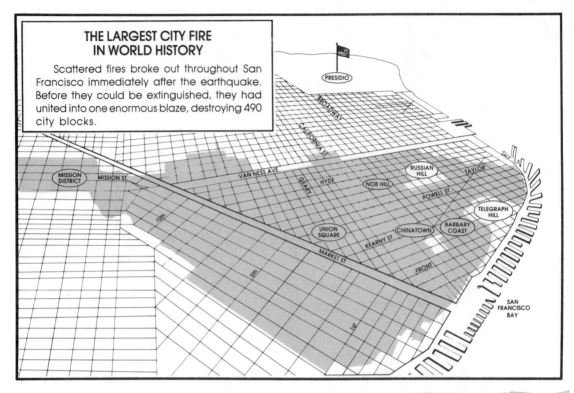

THE LARGEST CITY FIRE IN WORLD HISTORY

Scattered fires broke out throughout San Francisco immediately after the earthquake. Before they could be extinguished, they had united into one enormous blaze, destroying 490 city blocks.

Among them was the Mark Hopkins Art Institute that stood at the top of Nob Hill. All day Wednesday, students, faculty, and volunteers had worked to save the priceless paintings and sculptures housed in the Mark Hopkins Art Institute. They carried works to safety before the flames came too close to the building and the heat became too intense. Then the institute and its precious contents were left to the protection of the fire fighters.

Pumping from a cistern located under the pavement at California and Mason streets, the members of *3 Engine* tried to keep nearby buildings from igniting. When this water was used up, the fire fighters pumped the water from a cistern beneath the old mansion itself. The captain of *3 Engine* recalled what happened next:

While working there we were visited by His Honor the Mayor, who came up into the building to encourage us in our good work, and left orders to work our best in trying to save the Institute. Under the direction of Battalion Chief O'Brien, we continued working until the fire surrounded us in a very threatening manner, and to save our apparatus we had to leave there.

By Thursday morning, the institute was totally destroyed, and the fire fighters had retreated to Van Ness Avenue, the last great boulevard west of the fire. If the fire broke through at Van Ness, many believed the entire city would be consumed. All day Thursday, fire fighters dynamited buildings on the southern edge of Van Ness. They lit piles of rubble on fire, hoping to have burned away all possible fuel before the great fire arrived.

At one point, sparks from the fire crossed over Van Ness and ignited a stable. When this happened, some fire fighters, who had worked for thirty-six hours without stopping, began to cry. But the fire was quickly put out, as were other small flare-ups. The line at Van Ness held.

As the fires died down, many San Franciscans decided to leave the city. They crowded down Market Street to the Ferry Building to take the ferry across the bay to Oakland. Among the fleeing thousands was Enrico Caruso. The opera star and his valet, along with conductor Antonio Scotti paid a coachman three hundred dollars for a ride to the ferry landing, a trip that normally cost ten cents. When Caruso found himself at the end of a long, chaotic line, he approached the officials and asked to be allowed on the next departure. The officials laughed at him, then made the opera star sing a few bars of *Carmen* to prove his identity. The singer gave his second free concert in as many days and was permitted to go onto the next ferry. Once he left San Francisco, Caruso never returned.

Stalled by westerly breezes, the fire south of Market was also brought under control on Thursday. To the north, however, the fire that was stopped at Van Ness turned northward toward Russian Hill and Telegraph Hill. Residents there fought bravely to save their homes. They filled pots and pans with water drawn from old cisterns, then spread the water across their roofs with brooms, blankets, and gunny sacks. In the Italian District, some residents even broke open casks of wine and vinegar to douse the flames. These techniques worked, and many of the buildings on Russian Hill and Telegraph Hill were saved. By Saturday, the fire was out completely.

Five
Revival

When the *John A. Campbell* pulled into San Francisco, the crew was stunned. Instead of a brightly lit world of amusements and entertainment, they found the blackened shell of a city. Nearly 5 square miles (13 square kilometers), 490 city blocks, had burned. More than 28,000 buildings had been destroyed, including 30 schools and 80 churches. Gone were the fine restaurants, theaters, and libraries that had made San Francisco famous. Gone, too, were the saloons and night spots that sailors from the *John A. Campbell* had hoped to visit.

The blaze had been the largest city fire in the history of the world. It was one and one-half times as large as the famous Chicago Fire of 1871 and six times greater than the London Fire of 1666. More than 200,000 San Franciscans were homeless. At least 450 people were dead.

Many life-long residents could not even recognize the streets where their own homes had stood. James B. Stetson, who ran the California Street Railway Company, wrote:

> *I found it...very difficult to locate myself when wandering in the ruined district, as all the old landmarks are gone.*

Even before the fires were out, the city faced new problems. The soldiers who had been called into the city to maintain order became more and more disorderly. Many of them looted from the shops and liquor stores they were meant to protect. Others enforced the mayor's order to "shoot to kill" and asked no questions first. Witnesses described soldiers shooting—and even hanging—suspected looters. Some newspaper reporters estimated that of the 450 people who died during the fire, as many as 100 had been killed by the troops stationed in the city.

As the bodies of the dead lay in the streets, the danger of disease grew. General Funston's troops ordered citizens to help recover and bury the dead. Although the troops lacked the legal authority to enforce their orders, they did not lack the power to do so. They forced many civilians to work at bayonet point.

Albert Truelove was one of those who was forced to reclaim bodies. The sights were horrible, as Truelove explained:

> *Lots of the bodies had sort of melted. Eyes, hair, lips, ears, things like that were gone. Most of the dead were old. I guess they were people who hadn't the strength in them to run. But there were some young ones and children....*
>
> *In some of the buildings south of the Slot, the bodies had melted in with the general debris. You'd find a lump of fried flesh pitted with bits of iron, glass and other things. The smell was awful. You felt sick all the time.*

The deadly **bubonic plague** posed a serious threat after the fire. Although city officials had kept it a secret, several cases of bubonic plague had been reported in Chinatown in the weeks before the quake. The fleas that carry the disease live on rats, and the fire had driven these rats out of their nests in Chinatown and into all parts of the city. Truelove described the scene:

> *We got used to seeing hundreds of rats scampering across the ruins. The place looked like a rat paradise. For a bit of amusement, the soldier in charge of our gang would take a pot shot at a really big one if it was a little way away. Those that came right close got speared [with a bayonet]. By the end of the afternoon he was a real expert at spiking them.*

Marcus Herstein, a San Francisco doctor, warned the mayor and other city officials that an outbreak of bubonic plague was possible. Fearing that word of the plague would slow the city's rebuilding effort, Mayor Schmitz replied, "There is no plague." For months city officials tried to ignore the plague. By the time they acknowledged the problem, 160 San Franciscans had died of the disease.

Relief stations helped feed those left homeless by the quake and fire.

In the meantime, most city officials had turned their attention to feeding and sheltering the city's homeless. General Funston's wife had distributed a thousand of the presidio's army blankets and hundreds of tents to families even as the fire burned. Supplies from other forts poured into the city before the fire was out.

Emergency support flowed to the city from all over the world. A trainload of food, medical supplies, doctors, and nurses had arrived from Los Angeles before midnight on April 18. Los Angeles officials immediately sent Mayor Schmitz one hundred thousand dollars in cash—money that actually had been raised one week earlier for the relief of the victims of the Vesuvius eruption.

When word of the quake reached Ogden, Utah, all of the bakers in that town decided to help the victims of the disaster. For a week, every loaf of bread they baked went to San Francisco. Boys of the Chemewa Indian School in Oregon used their savings to bake 830 loaves of bread for San Francisco. The New York City Merchants Association sent fourteen boxcar loads of supplies. Along the way, the relief trains picked up boxcars bearing signs that read FOR SAN FRANCISCO—FROM DENVER, FROM BUFFALO, NEW YORK, FROM BURLINGTON, IOWA. More than $472,000 in aid was sent to San Francisco from foreign countries.

President Theodore Roosevelt ordered all money from foreign governments to be returned. He wanted the world to know that the United States could take care of its own people, although few Americans understood his decision. Roosevelt also ordered that all the aid collected—more than nine million dollars worth—be administered by the American Red Cross. This decision would firmly establish the Red Cross as the nation's leading disaster relief organization.

The Red Cross and the U.S. Army set up 150 relief stations throughout the city, including 27 hot food stations. They served as many as 315,000 meals a day for the next three weeks.

Cleanup began almost before the bricks had cooled. The owners of the Palace Hotel decided to tear down what was left of their once-magnificent building. They ended up paying crews ninety thousand dollars to haul away thirty million bricks. On May 1, two weeks after the earthquake, the city's Board of Public Works hired a crew of five thousand laborers to clear the upper part of Market Street. By May 5, the board hired a second crew of seventy-five hundred men to clean out lower Market, the Ferry Building, and all the nearby streets.

The cleanup proved so demanding that fifteen thousand **draft** horses were worked to death removing debris from the city. City officials decided to lay temporary railroad tracks on several streets so that the Southern Pacific Railroad could back open **gondola** cars into the city. Cleanup crews filled the gondola cars with debris. Steam locomotives pulled the cars out onto the loading docks that extended into the bay and dumped the rubble into the water.

Courtesy of The Bancroft Library

The brick pavement and trolley tracks on many streets had to be removed.

Some property owners delayed clearing their property. They feared that their insurance companies might refuse to pay their claims if the destroyed buildings were removed before the claims were settled.

Indeed, many insurance companies did everything they could to avoid paying the claims. Some declared **bankruptcy** immediately. Others claimed that buildings that were insured against fire had been destroyed by the earthquake before the fire swept through.

In the end, 80 percent of insurance claims were paid—a total of $229 million. This money formed the core of the rebuilding effort. On the Monday after the fire, three hundred plumbers went to work repairing the city's sewer and water lines.

Homeowners were also determined to rebuild, but in the meantime they needed places to live. Many wives and

Courtesy of The Bancroft Library

The Grand Opera House where Caruso had performed.

THE GREAT PLAN
THAT NOBODY FOLLOWED

In 1904, a group of San Francisco citizens calling themselves the Association for the Improvement and Adornment of San Francisco hired the famous architect and city planner, David H. Burnham, to draw plans for improving the city's layout. After more than a year of work, Burnham presented his ideas to the association. He proposed that wide boulevards be carved into the city's hills, replacing the steepest streets. He suggested widening other streets and extending the panhandle of Golden Gate Park out to the docks.

But most people did not have the patience to wait for any plan. They ignored the recommendations of the association and set about rebuilding their city much as it had been built before—with no city plan to guide them. The city plan has since been all but forgotten.

---

children left the city and spent the summer with relatives and friends. Other families moved in with San Franciscans whose homes had not been damaged. In the fall, the city decided to build six thousand three-room cottages for the refugees. The cottages were built in six locations, or camps, around the city. Three of the camps were located in Golden Gate Park.

With much of their city in ruins, many San Franciscans urged their fellow citizens to use the rebuilding as an opportunity to improve their city. They wanted to adopt a blueprint that would help the city prepare for future growth. Most building owners, however, were more interested in their immediate needs than the beauty of the city. James D. Phelan, a San Francisco businessman whose uninsured $1 million office building was destroyed in the fire, put it this way:

> *San Francisco is not an ancient city. It was the recent creation of the Pioneers and possessed the...stores of only a couple of generations. Its temples, monuments and public buildings were not of conspicuous merit or of great value. There was... nothing destroyed that cannot be speedily rebuilt.*

Buildings were erected on the same spots where old structures had fallen. New buildings were erected on the rubble that had been dumped into the bay, making these structures as vulnerable to earthquake damage as the ones that had been built on the loose fill dirt above Mission and Willow Creeks. The plan for an electric trolley system, hated by many San Franciscans because of the spider web of overhead wires it would bring, was hastily approved.

By the end of 1906, many new homes and dozens of new office buildings were completed. Demand for space in the new buildings was tremendous. A story in the *Overland Express* described the frenzy:

> *Whenever a new building is started, all the flats are rented before the foundation is laid.... Prospective tenants who hear of a building being let, trace up the contractor, interview the owner, and pay a deposit on the flat before the building operations are commenced.*

Within three years, 20,000 new buildings had replaced the 28,000 destroyed in the earthquake and fire. By then, it took an expert to find the barest traces of California's greatest natural disaster.

Six
Recurrence

After surviving the most destructive earthquake in California history, thousands of San Franciscans began rebuilding on land they knew might begin pitching and buckling again at any time. Why did they do it? Why didn't they just find a safer place to live?

For many San Franciscans, it was an economic decision. The city still had one of the best natural harbors on the West Coast. The wharves and waterfront district were practically untouched by the quake and fire. The shipping merchants could resume work almost immediately. They were not about to abandon their thriving businesses.

Also, pioneer spirit still guided many people's decisions in 1906. Many of them had seen San Francisco built in a matter of decades, and they believed it could be built again. Besides, they had just survived the city's worst disaster. What more did they have to fear? As the decades have passed since 1906, that question has haunted San Franciscans and a growing number of Californians.

Seismologists, scientists who study earthquakes, now tell us that California rests on the border of two major **tectonic plates**. In addition, fault lines capable of unleashing violent earthquakes crisscross much of the state. What would happen if an earthquake like the one of 1906 struck one of California's densely populated areas today?

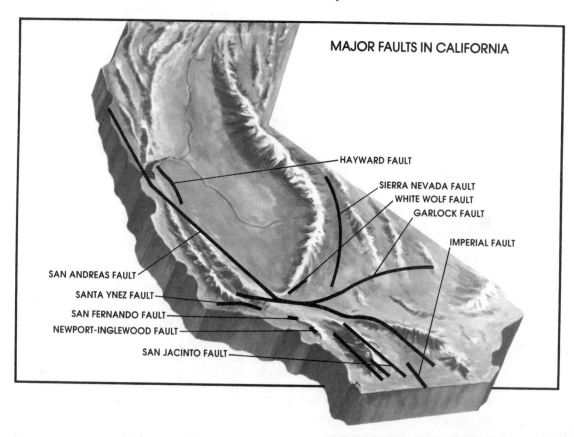

MAJOR FAULTS IN CALIFORNIA

HAYWARD FAULT
SIERRA NEVADA FAULT
WHITE WOLF FAULT
GARLOCK FAULT
IMPERIAL FAULT
SAN ANDREAS FAULT
SANTA YNEZ FAULT
SAN FERNANDO FAULT
NEWPORT-INGLEWOOD FAULT
SAN JACINTO FAULT

WILL CALIFORNIA BECOME AN ISLAND IN THE PACIFIC?

Evidence gathered by hundreds of scientists shows that millions of years from now, part of the California coast could become an island or a group of islands in the Pacific Ocean. This is based on the theory of *continental drift*, in which the continents of the world are believed to be moving a few inches every year.

The force behind this continental drift is plate tectonics, the movement of the plates that make up the earth's crust. The California coast lies directly over the edges of two plates, which are pushing against one another. California is on the continental plate, and the Pacific Ocean is on the oceanic plate.

What causes these plates to move? At the bottom of the world's oceans, volcanic activity pushes molten rock from the mantle up to the earth's crust. As it hardens, this new crust pushes the old crust away in both directions, causing the plates to move.

But the plates are not getting larger. Where they meet, the edge of the oceanic plate is being forced underneath the continental plate. This forms a deep trench, known as a *subduction trench*, along the ocean floor. The rock that is forced under melts and becomes part of the mantle. In this way, the earth's crust is gradually recycled.

In 1988, the California Department of Conservation investigated what could happen if a portion of the Hayward Fault, which runs through the Bay Area cities of Hayward, Fremont, Oakland, and Berkeley, were to rupture. Officials estimated that the strongest shock on this fault would measure about 7.5 on the **Richter scale**. An earthquake of this **magnitude** would kill 1,500 to 4,500 people and injure more than 50,000.

The San Andreas Fault could generate an even stronger shock. This fault runs not only through San Francisco, but also extends through much of the state including heavily populated sections of Los Angeles and Orange counties. A report issued by the federal government in 1980 estimated the damage that would be caused in Los Angeles if an earthquake with a magnitude of 8.3 was centered near Los Angeles.

The report concluded that such a quake would cause $25 billion in damage. At least 52,000 people would be left homeless. The number of deaths would depend on the time of day that the earthquake struck. If it occurred during peak business hours, as many as 12,500 people would be killed and at least 50,000 people would be injured.

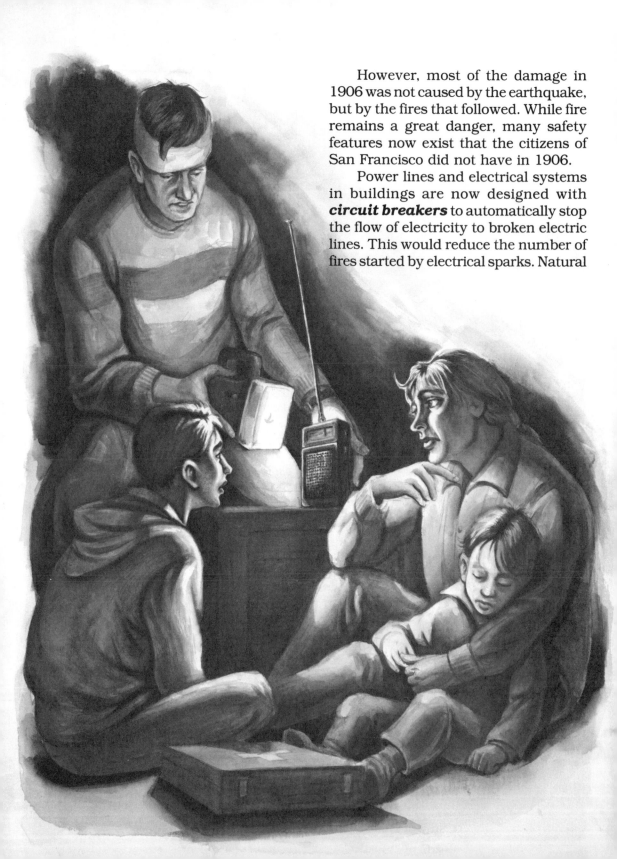

However, most of the damage in 1906 was not caused by the earthquake, but by the fires that followed. While fire remains a great danger, many safety features now exist that the citizens of San Francisco did not have in 1906.

Power lines and electrical systems in buildings are now designed with *circuit breakers* to automatically stop the flow of electricity to broken electric lines. This would reduce the number of fires started by electrical sparks. Natural gas pipelines also contain automatic shut-off systems in case of breaks or leaks, reducing the potential of fires.

Water mains are now built with flexible joints that move as the earth shakes, improving the chances that they will survive a major quake. If they break, water-pressure meters will allow officials to quickly pinpoint breaks in water lines. Backhoes and other heavy-duty digging equipment would enable workers to repair damage quickly.

Ironically, a smaller quake could be even more destructive if it were centered directly under Los Angeles. According to a 1985 report by the United States Geological Survey, an earthquake measuring 7.5, only one-eighth as strong as the San Francisco earthquake, could kill between 4,400 and 21,000 people, if it occurred on the Newport-Inglewood Fault, which runs between the Los Angeles airport and the downtown area. A major quake on this fault would injure between 18,000 and 84,000 people and leave 192,000 homeless. The cost of damage would be $62 billion.

Most experts agree that the damage caused by future earthquakes will be great. But many believe that fewer lives will be lost than in the 1906 earthquake. For one thing, emergency radio broadcasts will alert people to locations of fires, floods, downed power lines, ruined roadways, and unstable buildings.

Advances in architecture may also save lives. Many structures built in California after the San Francisco Earthquake include safety features to make them resistant to earthquake damage. Many of the tallest buildings are anchored deep into the earth with steel foundations, much as the Palace Hotel

Courtesy of Transamerica Corporation

BUILDING TO WITHSTAND EARTHQUAKES

The Transamerica Pyramid in San Francisco is one example of a building designed to withstand a major earthquake. The triangular *trusses* and steel columns that form the building's foundation will absorb much of the shock of an earthquake. That and the unique shape of the structure will reduce swaying, which causes buildings to collapse. This is only one of the innovations in design and construction that architects and engineers hope will make our cities safer in future earthquakes.

was in 1906. Theoretically, these buildings would not collapse. Instead, they would sway like trees as the earth shifted beneath them. Newer buildings are designed with special shock absorbing features to reduce the vibration from an earthquake.

Fire fighters have also benefited from modern technology. Helicopters and radio equipment allow fire fighters to survey a situation and direct their efforts more effectively than could the San Francisco fire department of 1906. Aircraft can be used to dump water on the flames. In San Francisco, a saltwater pumping system built after the 1906 earthquake can be used to provide fire fighters with seawater should the water mains in the city fail again.

Technology could also speed disaster relief efforts. Satellite communications and air transportation would allow relief agencies to rush medical personnel and supplies to earthquake victims much more quickly. Hospitals that are damaged could use ambulances and automobiles to move patients to undamaged facilities with greater speed than in the past.

Not everyone believes that improved technology will prevail in a major earthquake. In its 1980 report, the U.S. government predicted that "response to such an earthquake would become disorganized and largely ineffective." This is because technology itself is especially vulnerable to earthquake damage. Without electrical power, computerized emergency and communi-

cations systems of all kinds would fail.

Computer and communications failures could combine to produce an economic disaster that would have been unthinkable in 1906. Since San Francisco and Los Angeles are world banking centers, the destruction of computing systems in these cities could trigger worldwide financial chaos. Banks, stock exchanges, and international corporations would be cut off from critical electronic communication.

In the days following a major earthquake in San Francisco or Los Angeles, the financial chaos might lead to panic. Fearing bank closures, people might try to withdraw their funds from California banks. Stockholders of California companies would be unable to resume business after the earthquake. Insurance companies would also have to sell a great deal of their stock to pay for the damage in California. All these stock sales could cause a major drop in stock market prices.

A major earthquake in California could also affect the state's farming industry. Since California is the nation's largest food producer, food shortages could be expected nationwide. This would drive food prices up and increase the nation's financial difficulties.

Whether pessimistic or optimistic about the outcome of a major earthquake, there is no way to test these predictions. The fact is, no one knows how well or how poorly technology will function in the next major California earthquake. But there is one thing that nearly everyone agrees upon: there will be another major California earthquake.

Nearly ten million Californians live close enough to major fault lines that their lives could be endangered by an earthquake. Many scientists believe that even a few minutes' warning before a major quake could save thousands of lives.

It would allow people to seek earthquake shelters, allow fire fighters to move their equipment out of vulnerable firehouses, and even allow computer operators to save important data before it is wiped out by a power failure.

Scientists are currently working on several theories and methods that could unlock the mystery of earthquake predictions.

Geologists Robert Wesson and Craig Nicholson analyzed the cyclical nature of major earthquakes in California. In 1985, they published a list of sixteen locations where they predicted earthquakes larger than the 1906 quake in San Francisco would occur between 1986 and 1996. In 1987, one of the sixteen predicted earthquakes occurred in

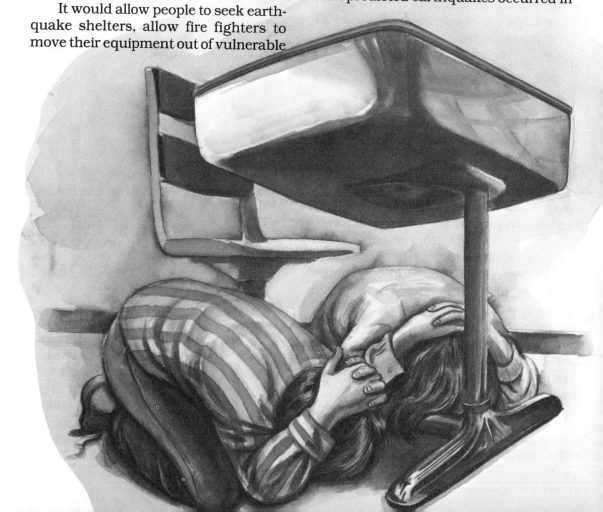

PREDICTING EARTHQUAKES

Seismologists are now able to predict quite accurately where major earthquakes are likely to occur. And they are using new methods to predict when a quake will happen.

Creepmeters (shown above) are used to detect minute movement of land near a fault. *Gravimeters* check changes in the *density* of the ground, which indicates the movement of rock beneath the surface.

Space technology is also being used to predict earthquakes. Lasers positioned on opposite sides of a fault beam light to a satellite in space. The beams are reflected off the satellite and back to earth. Incredibly small changes in the angle and travel time of these laser beams can be recorded and used to pinpoint movements along a fault line.

Many other scientists are observing animal behavior as a way to predict earthquakes. And in China, where earthquakes occur frequently, scientists have often observed strange animal behavior just before a violent quake. Cows and horses refuse to enter their pens, dogs howl, birds screech, rats run around in circles, and frogs jump out of ponds.

Whatever the reason, animals do seem to sense an earthquake before people do. By evacuating cities and villages whenever these strange animal behaviors are observed, officials in China have saved thousands of lives.

the sparsely populated Superstition Hills region. Three others have occurred since in predicted locations, but they measured less than 5.7 on the Richter scale.

While scientists have greatly increased their knowledge of how, why, and where an earthquake will occur, the ability to predict exactly when it will occur still eludes them. However, with the aid of sensitive instruments to detect movement of the earth's crust, and with the use of lasers and satellites to measure and time these movements, and with the scientific study of animal behavior, they hope to give the people of California a few precious minutes of warning.

Whether or not the warnings come in time, how people react to the next major earthquake, how much damage it will cause, and how many lives will be lost are all uncertain. What is certain is that sooner or later, the spirit and will of California's inhabitants will be tested again, as it was in San Francisco in 1906.

Glossary

bankruptcy . . . . To be unable to pay one's debts and legally freed from doing so. Financial ruin.

brothel . . . . A house of prostitution.

bubonic plague . . . . [byoo-**BON**-ick **PLAYG**] A deadly disease that is carried to humans by fleas from infected rats.

circuit breaker . . . . [**SIR**-kit] An automatic switch that stops the flow of electric current through wires when dangerously high amounts of current flow through suddenly.

cistern . . . . A tank for storing water, especially rainwater.

clapboard . . . . A board used for siding on the outside of a wooden house. One edge is thinner than the other so that one board can overlap another for a tight fit.

concussion . . . . A violent shaking.

conflagration . . . . [con-fluh-**GRAY**-shun] A large fire that does great damage.

continental drift . . . . The theory in which the continents of the world are believed to be moving a few inches every year.

creepmeter . . . . An instrument used to detect movement of land near a fault.

crust . . . . The surface, or outermost layer of the earth mostly made up of hard rock.

density . . . . The ratio of a material's mass to its volume or size. For example, solid rock is more dense than sand.

draft . . . . Suited for pulling heavy loads.

ethnic . . . . Having to do with the culture, history, and customs of a nationality or race.

facade . . . . [fuh-**SOD**] The face or front of a building.

fault . . . . A crack or fracture caused by the movement of tectonic plates in the earth's crust.

firebreak . . . . An area in the path of a fire which is cleared of fuel to limit the spread of the fire.

focus . . . . The point of origin of an earthquake.

fresco . . . . The art of painting with watercolors on wet plaster.

gable . . . . The triangle formed in a wall of a building by the sloping edges of a ridged roof.

geologist . . . . One who studies the earth's crust and its layers.

gondola . . . . [**GON**-duh-luh] A railroad freight car with low sides and no top.

gravimeter . . . . [gruh-**VIM**-uh-ter] An instrument used to measure density.

ignition point . . . . The temperature at which a material catches fire.

immigrant . . . . One who leaves a country to settle permanently in another.

inner core . . . . The mass of solid iron which forms the center of the earth.

loot . . . . To steal or rob.

magnitude . . . . Size or extent.

mantle . . . . The layer of molten rock which covers the outer core of the center of the earth.

outer core . . . . The liquid layer of molten iron which covers the inner core of the earth.

plate . . . . One of several large, moving sections of the earth's crust.

presidio . . . . A military post.

Richter scale . . . . A scale for measuring the strength of an earthquake.

seismic waves . . . . The various waves of energy which move out in every direction following an earthquake.

seismologist . . . . A scientist who studies earthquakes.

subduction trench . . . . A deep trench along the ocean floor where the oceanic plate is being forced underneath the continental plate.

tam . . . . A Scottish cap with a round, flat top. Short for tam-o'-shanter.

tectonic . . . . Pertaining to changes in the earth's crust.

tremor . . . . A quick shaking or vibrating of the earth's surface.

truss . . . . The wood or metal framework used to support a roof.

tunic . . . . A blouse or jacket that reaches to the hips and is often worn with a belt.

turret . . . . A small tower on a building, usually at a corner.

undulate . . . . [**UN**-joo-late] To rise and fall in waves.

Victorian . . . . A heavily ornamented style of architecture made popular in England in the 1800s.

villa . . . . A large, showy house in the country.

Further Reading

SAN FRANCISCO EARTHQUAKE

Bronson, William. *The Earth Shook, The Sky Burned*. Garden City, N.Y.: Doubleday & Co., 1959.

Everett, Marshall. *The Complete Story of the San Francisco Earthquake*. Chicago: Bible House, 1906.

Stein, R. Conrad. *The Story of the San Francisco Earthquake*. Chicago: Children's Press, 1983.

HISTORY OF SAN FRANCISCO & CALIFORNIA

Lewis, Oscar. *The Story of California*. Garden City, N.Y.: Garden City Books, 1955.

Muscatine, Doris. *Old San Francisco*. New York: Putnam, 1975.

Stull, Edity. *The Story of California: A Short History of the Golden State*. New York: Grosset and Dunlop, 1968.

EARTHQUAKES

Halacy, D.S. Jr. *Earthquakes: A Natural History*. Indianapolis and New York: Bobbs-Merrill Co., 1974.

Iacopi, Robert. *Earthquake Country*. Menlo Park, Calif.: Lane Publishing Co., 1971.

Steinbrugge, Karl V. *Earthquakes, Volcanoes, and Tsunamis*. New York: Skandia, 1982.

Walker, Bryce. *Earthquake*. Alexandria, Va.: Time-Life Books, 1982.

FIRES AND FIRE FIGHTING

Blumberg, Rhoda. *Firefighters*. New York: Franklin Watts, 1976.

Colby, C.B. *Space Age Fire Fighters: New Weapons in the Fireman's Arsenal*. New York: Coward, McCann & Geoghegan, 1973.

Da Costa, Phil. *100 Years of America's Fire Fighting Apparatus*. Los Angeles: Floyd Clymer Publications, 1964.

Dean, Anabel. *Fire! How Do They Fight It?* Philadelphia: Westminster Press, 1978.

Hatmon, Paul W. *Yesterday's Fire Engines*. Minneapolis, Minn.: Lerner Publications Co., 1980.

Holden, Raymond. *All About Fire*. New York: Random House, 1964.

Smith, Dennis, and Jill Freedman. *Firehouse*. Garden City, N.Y.: Doubleday & Co., 1977.

Other Works Consulted

Caughey, John W. *California, History of a Remarkable State.* Englewood Cliffs, N.J.: Prentice Hall, 1982.

Colombo, John Robert. *The Great San Francisco Earthquake and Fire.* Fredericton, N.B., Canada: Fiddlehead Poetry Books, 1936.

Kahn, Edgar M. *Cable Car Days in San Francisco.* Stanford, Calif.: Stanford Univ. Press, 1940.

Lavender, David. *California: Land of New Beginnings.* New York: Harper & Row, 1972.

Lotchin, Roger W. *San Francisco, 1846-1856.* New York: Oxford Univ. Press, 1974.

Morris, Charles. *The San Francisco Calamity by Earthquake and Fire.* Secaucus, N.J.: Citadel Press, 1986.

Thomas, Gordon and Max Morgan Witts. *The San Francisco Earthquake.* New York: Stein and Day, 1971.

Index

Co-author James House has been a writer and editor for several West Coast newspapers. He holds a masters degree in English Literature from the University of California at Davis, and is co-director of Learning Development Services in San Diego, California.

Co-author Bradley Steffens has published numerous poems and plays in more than thirty literary journals and has received many awards for his writing. This is his fourth book.

Illustrations designed by Maurie Manning capture the drama of the events described in this book.

Manning majored in illustration at Massachusetts College of Art in Boston and has been a professional children's illustrator for more than six years. Her work appears regularly in such magazines as *Children's Digest, Humpty Dumpty,* and *Highlights for Children.*

Manning was assisted by a team of three artists: Michael Spackman, Robert Caldwell, and Randol Eagles. A professional painter for more than nineteen years, Michael Spackman received his training at the High Museum Academy of Art in Atlanta. Robert Caldwell, a graduate of Syracuse University with a degree in fine arts, has been a fine arts professional for eight years. Randol Eagles is a specialist in figurative illustration, and has been a professional illustrator for three years.

Photography Credits

Photo on page 36 courtesy of
The Fine Arts Museums of San Francisco,
Achenbach Foundation for Graphic Arts

Photo on page 53 courtesy of
Transamerica Corporation

Photo on page 33 courtesy of
Stanford University Library

Photos on pages 31, 46, 47, and 48 courtesy of
The Bancroft Library